THE
COWARD'S
ALMANAC

By Marvin Kitman

The Coward's Almanac, or The Yellow Pages
The Marvin Kitman TV Show
George Washington's Expense Account (with Gen.
   George Washington)
You Can't Tell a Book by Its Cover
The Red Chinese Air Force Diet, Exercise and
   Sex Manual (Translation, under Pseudonym:
   William Randolph Hirsch, with Victor Navasky
   and Richard Lingeman)
The Number-One Best Seller

by Marvin Kitman

drawings by LouMyers

DOUBLEDAY & COMPANY, INC.

THE
COWARD'S ALMANAC
Or The Yellow Pages

Garden City, New York   1975

Library of Congress Cataloging in Publication Data

Kitman, Marvin, 1929–
　The coward's almanac.

　1. Fear—Anecdotes, facetiae, satire, etc.　I. Title.　II. Title: The
yellow pages.
PN6231.F4K57　　818'.5'407
ISBN 0-385-06467-5
Library of Congress Catalog Card Number 75–116221

A number of people have made contributions to this work even greater than mine but are too cowardly to have their names listed as co-authors. The best parts of this book were written by Richard Lingeman, Mark Schubin, Gerald Nachman, Victor Navasky, and Susan Edmiston. This acknowledgment is what the law means by the phrase "credit by association." All the pusillanimous contributors stand behind everything written in these pages—very far behind.

Anon.
c/o General Delivery
New Jersey

THE
COWARD'S
ALMANAC

JANUARY 1

X ray of a Coward's Nervous System

JANUARY 2

The discovery of phobias by the psychiatrists has done much to clear the atmosphere. Whereas in the old days a person would say: "Let's get the heck out of here!" today he says: "Let's get the heck out of here! I've got claustrophobia."

Most everybody knows the name of the phobia that he has personally, and it is a great comfort to him. If he is afraid of high places, he just says, "Oh, it's just my old acrophobia," and jumps.

If he is afraid of being alone, he knows that he has monophobia and has the satisfaction of knowing that he is a pathological case. If he keeps worrying, in the middle of a meal, about the possibility of being buried alive, he can flatter himself that he has taphophobia, and that it is no worse than a bad cold.

But there are some honeys among the phobias that don't get much publicity. There is, for example, phobophobia, which is the fear of having a phobia, even though you may not have one at the moment. This takes the form of the patient sitting in terror and saying to himself: "Supposing I should be afraid of food, I would starve to death!" Not a very pretty picture, you will admit.

Then there is kemophobia, or the fear of sitting too close to the edge of the chair and falling off. People with kemophobia are constantly hitching themselves back in their chairs until they tip themselves over backward. This gives them the same general effect as falling off the chair frontward, so they find themselves in a cul-de-sac.

Then there is goctophobia, or fear of raising the hand to strike oneself in the face, with the possibility of putting an eye out. These patients keep their hands in their pockets all the time and have to be fed by paid attendants. A nasty complication arises when they also have nictophobia, or fear of paid attendants.

Some of the other little-known phobias are octophobia, or

fear of the figure 8; genophobia, or the fear of being burned on door handles; kneebophobia, or the fear that one knee is going to bend backwards instead of forwards some day; and optophobia, or the dread of opening the eyes for fear of what they will see.

Tell us your phobias and we will tell you what you are afraid of.

ROBERT BENCHLEY

JANUARY 4

The First Coward

Archeological discoveries have revealed that primitive man had a bone spur on his heels, so-called high-heeled man. This made it impossible for him to move in a backward direction. Thus, primitive man always stood up and fought. Then about 10,000,-000 B.C. so-called round-heeled man appeared (*Pithecanthropus protectus*), who invented the technique of retreating. As the round-heeled man lived to run away another day, he survived the evolutionary process, while spur-heeled man became extinct. The quaint habit of knights and cowboys wearing high heels and spurs is a last-remaining vestige of the ancient race of man.

JANUARY 5

THE SPORTING LIFE: What is the highest mountain climbed by a coward?
ANSWER: Washington Heights.

JANUARY 8

Whistles in the Dark

"A coward is a hero with a wife, kids and a mortgage."

JANUARY 10

What Are You—a Coward?

Take this simple in-depth personality test and find out.*

*Warning: If you're afraid to find out, don't take this test.

Agree   *Not Sure*

1. Sometimes I feel sad for no reason.
2. My favorite color is yellow.
3. If I cover my head with blankets, nothing can harm me (I hope).
4. Large, fierce police dogs have it in for me.
5. I would throw all this up and go seek my future in Brazil if I didn't have sinus trouble.
6. Revolving doors have it in for me.
7. Better safe than sorry.
8. ABC means always be careful.
9. I am seriously worried that the birds are plotting something.
10. Sanitation men have it in for me.
11. Somewhere, right now, a big computer is looking for my card.

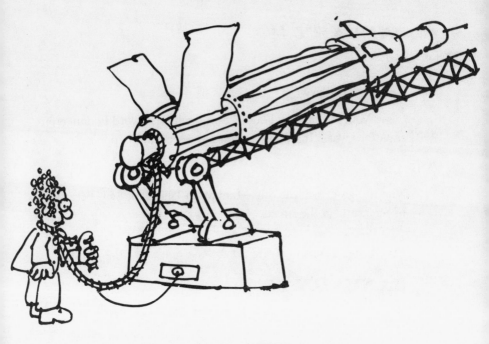

Agree   *Not Sure*

12. The CIA has decided I am the only American qualified to carry out a suicide mission.

13. In reality, pop-top beer cans are not as safe as they make them out to be.

14. I have a routine blood test; my doctor will discover that I have tertiary syphilis.

15. A big bad wolf is to be feared.

16. They have it in for me.

SCORING: Score one point for each question answered correctly. If you're afraid you didn't answer any correctly, you're probably right. A real coward would be afraid to take this test.

JANUARY 11

Coward's Gallery

"The Man in the Grey Flannel Suit," whose byword in dangerous situations was, "It will be interesting to see what happens."

The Indian brave who sold Manhattan Island for $24. Because of the crime in the streets.

JANUARY 14

(Benedict Arnold's birthday)

JANUARY 16

The Coward's Consultant

Dear Arnold:

An old man ran up to me in the street one night and told me his wife was being mugged in the alley. I offered him a dime to call the police. Did I do the right thing?

—Frightened

Dear Frightened:

Yes, but if you could have directed him to a call box, you could have saved the dime.

JANUARY 17

The Coward's Consultant

Dear Arnold:

An old man ran up to me in the street one night and told me his wife was being mugged in an alley. I told him I was a physician and we're not allowed to interfere. Did I do the right thing?

—Frightened, M.D.

Dear Frightened:

Yes. However, you might have also pointed out that your malpractice insurance had lapsed.

JANUARY 19

This is a good day to bring all your zippers in for their annual checkup.

JANUARY 22

The First Man to Throw in the Towel

Alfonso ("El Pollo") Carlos Diaz y Serrano (1843–87)

JANUARY 25

Ins and Outs of Cowardice (should be read like planting tables in the *Farmer's Almanac*)

DATE	WHAT'S IN
Jan. 1–Feb. 19	Claustrophobia
Feb. 2–Mar. 21	Hydrophobia
Mar. 14–June 30	Brontephobia*
May 15–July 10	Acrophobia
July 21–Aug. 7	Have No Fears
Aug. 1–Aug. 28	Thalassa Crusophobia
Sept. 8–Sept. 30	Ophidiophobia**
Aug. 20–Oct. 15	Nyctophobia***
Sept. 9–Nov. 12	Phthisiophobia****
Nov. 8–Dec. 9	Ophidionyctophthisiophobia*****
Dec. 1–Dec. 2	Ergophobia******
Dec. 3–Dec. 19	Calorphobia*******
Dec. 13–Dec. 21	Gatophobia********

* Fear of Charlotte, Anne and Emily Brontë.

** Fear of snakes.

*** Fear of the Dark.

**** Fear of tuberculosis.

***** Fear of snakes in the dark carrying tuberculosis.

****** "I am; therefore I fear."

******* Fear of heat in kitchen (example of use: if you have calorphobia, get out).

******** Gatophobia is the fear of cats. Katzophobia is the fear of Katz.

JANUARY 27

Cruise Time

Hold an abandon ship drill today!

FEBRUARY 1

(Chinese New Year's Day)

This is the Year of the Chicken Dragon.

FEBRUARY 2

Today is Ground Hog Day—a good day to be afraid of your own shadow.

FEBRUARY 3

Basic Fears

Basic Fear #1—Fear of biting down on a scrap of tin-foil.

Basic Fear #2—Fear of not being invited to any New Year's Eve parties.

Basic Fear #3—Fear of screaming "Fire!" in a crowded theater.

Basic Fear #4—Fear of going into advertising.

Basic Fear #5—Fear of not finding footnotes.

Basic Fear #6—Fear that no one but relatives will show up at your funeral.

Basic Fear #7—Fear of being caught in cross fire during a shoot-out in a crowded department store.

Basic Fear #8—Fear of stepping up to a bank teller on the spur of the moment and writing a hold-up note on your deposit slip.

Basic Fear #9—Fear of New York taxi drivers.

Basic Fear #10—Fear of New York.

Basic Fear ♯11—Fear of not getting any of the references in a foreign film, such as the symbolism, allusions.

Basic Fear ♯12—Fear of losing your mind.

Basic Fear ♯13—Fear of House Ways and Means Committee.

Basic Fear ♯14—Fear of shoe clerk finding holes in your socks.

Basic Fear ♯15—Fear of running away with a manicurist and you bite your nails.

Basic Fear ♯16—Fear of Turkish baths.

Basic Fear ♯17—Fear of **Dr. Martin Abend.**

Basic Fear ♯18—Fear that the shifty-eyed guy who asked you for a match was a pyromaniac.

Basic Fear ♯19—Fear of missing the point of dirty jokes.

Basic Fear ♯20—Fear of your accountant cheating you on your income tax.

Basic Fear ♯21—Fear of someone else using your toothbrush.

Basic Fear ♯22—Fear of losing the cap from the toothpaste.

Basic Fear ♯23—Fear that your wife's brother will steal your credit cards and blow all your money on the Riviera.

Basic Fear ♯24—Fear of burning your finger while poking inside a toaster with a knife to retrieve a chunk of burning bagel.

Basic Fear ♯25—Fear that you'll swallow the thermometer and die of mercury poisoning.

Basic Fear ♯26—Fear of nuclear annihilation.

Basic Fear ♯27—Fear of kissing your dentist or optometrist during an examination.

Basic Fear ♯28—Fear of your dentist or optometrist kissing *you.*

Basic Fear ♯29—Fear of becoming an avid viewer of "The New Treasure Hunt."

Basic Fear ♯30—Fear of coffee being spilled on you by a stewardess and having to marry the girl.

Basic Fear ♯31—Fear of calling a Negro "black" or vice versa.

Basic Fear ♯32—Fear of being hit by a cab in Times Square when not wearing panties.

Basic Fear ♯33—Fear of not remembering first-aid procedures in an emergency.

Basic Fear #34—Fear of being unable to keep from ripping off your clothes in the public library.

Basic Fear #35—Fear of not finding a husband in college.

Basic Fear #36—Fear of having accomplished nothing significant by age thirty.

Basic Fear #37—Fear of having accomplished nothing significant by age forty.

Basic Fear #38—Fear of accomplishing something not worth accomplishing.

Basic Fear #39—Fear of falling into a hole in the fourth dimension and being lost forever.

Basic Fear #40—Fear of your State Farm man.

Basic Fear #41—Fear of your car's horn blowing at a funeral and being unable to stop it.

Basic Fear #42—Fear of being kidnaped and no one will pay ransom.

Basic Fear #43—Fear of a Red Chinese invasion of Staten Island.

Basic Fear ⚹44—Fear of being prosecuted by District Attorney Jim Garrison for Kennedy's assassination.

Basic Fear ⚹45—Fear of cutting your finger on the flap of an envelope.

Basic Fear ⚹46—Fear of being kidnaped by the S.L.A.

Basic Fear ⚹47—Fear of not receiving any Christmas cards.

Basic Fear ⚹48—Fear of never being sick a day in your life. only to be struck down in your prime by a rare incurable disease.

Basic Fear ⚹49—Fear of not fearing the number 13, black cats, cracked mirrors, open umbrellas, shoes or hats on a bed, spilled salt, etc.

Basic Fear ⚹50—Fear of eating a potato knish spiked with LSD.

Basic Fear ⚹51—Fear of falling over backwards.

Basic Fear ⚹52—Fear of eating yourself into an early grave.

Basic Fear ⚹53—Fear of marrying your long-lost mother.

Basic Fear ⚹54—Fear that God is dead, when he only may be in semiretirement in a condominium in Miami Beach.

Basic Fear ⚹55—Fear of Andy Warhol movies.

Basic Fear ⚹56—Fear of being picked up in an Andy Warhol movie by a person whose sex you aren't sure of.

Basic Fear ⚹57—Fear of latent homosexuality.

Basic Fear ✕58—Fear of latent heterosexuality.
Basic Fear ✕59—Fear of latent bisexuality.
Basic Fear ✕60—Fear of latent asexuality.
Basic Fear ✕61—Fear of falling in love with Martha Mitchell.
Basic Fear ✕62—Fear of not finishing the Sunday paper.

FEBRUARY 5

Reader's Digest **Version of the 62 Basic Fears**

Fear:
. . . anything that moves.
. . . anything that doesn't.
. . . anything else.

And you can never go wrong.

(Please clip and post on your shaving mirror. Don't cut yourself.)

FEBRUARY 6

Coward's Business Page

Corporate president's fears.

1. Arousing Ralph Nader's interest.
2. Latest market quotations.

Don't read unless you are on the first floor.

FEBRUARY 9

Anatomy of a Coward (Inside and Out)

Hair standing on end
Glass jaw (sometimes chattering)
Chattering teeth
Chicken (or pigeon) heart
Jellyfish spine (sometimes spineless)
Creeping flesh
Trembling hands
Gutless
Lily liver
Yellow belly (often streaked)
Blood running cold in veins
Knees of jelly
Tail (now extinct) between legs
Cold feet
Curling toes

FEBRUARY 13 (FRIDAY)

A typical apartment, showing the safest places for social cowards to be at cocktail parties.

1) Closet.
2) Master bedroom, where you can scan the photographs of the host's kids.
3) Rubber plant: good to hide behind.
4) Bathroom: bad for late in the party, unless there are more than one.
5) Fire escape: good for hasty exits.
6) Under couch or bed, unless there are pets.
7) On ceiling.
8) Outside.

FEBRUARY 14

(St. Valentine's Day)

The invention of closing the eyes while kissing, April 7, 1923.
The invention of the invalid mother (for avoiding marriage),
　January 2, 1897.
The invention of the chaperone, November 12, 1784.
The invention of the previous engagement, January 19, 1911.
The invention of arranged marriages, blind dates, dancing class
　and pen pals, 1870–1909.
The invention of the roommate (unknown).
The invention of the headache, October 13, 1949.
The invention of the period (see Genesis, Old Testament).
The invention of the VD movie, December 7, 1941.

FEBRUARY 22

(George Washington's Real Birthday)

Don't get worked up about the change of holidays. George
Washington would have liked to have two birthdays.

Things to fear today:
—Fear of crossing rivers.
—Fear of a national paternity suit for being father of a country.
—Fear of the credibility gap.

FEBRUARY 29

Fear of not being sure that today isn't March 1.

MARCH 3

The worst thing that can happen is that the plane will crash.
—An old American saying

The fear of dying on a plane is an irrational one. A scientist helps calm fears with a few hard facts.

Q. Where, in a scientific sense, is the best place to sit in a plane in the unlikely event of a crash?
A. Either in the front or the back is safer, though I prefer the front, where such authorities as the pilots sit.

Q. Do planes, on impact with the ground, break open in one, two, or three places?
A. Yes.

Q. Why don't airplanes carry parachutes for the passengers?
A. The added weight would add to the possibility of a crash.

Q. Why do they carry them for the crew?
A. A good pilot is hard to find.

Q. Since they probably wouldn't want to be seen in the air terminal cocktail lounge, where do the pilots do their drinking?
A. In the cockpit, or in the hangar.

Q. Why do you have no fear of flight yourself?
A. I take the train.

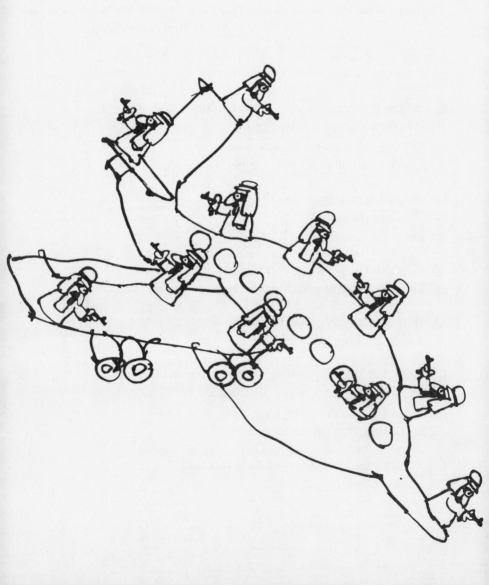

MARCH 4

Airline Fears

—Fear of sitting next to a hijacker.
—Fear of sitting next to an air marshal.
- -Fear of sitting between a hijacker and an air marshal.
—Fear of someone collecting on the flight insurance you bought.
—Fear of an overhead plane emptying its washrooms on you.

MARCH 10

Some of the Dangers of Air Travel

—Getting in an automobile accident on your way to the airport.

—Getting mugged in the waiting room.

—Tripping while boarding the plane (does not apply to drug users).

—Starving.

—Overeating.

—Being sterilized by the microwaves from the plane's microwave oven.

—Burning your retina by looking at the sun through your window.

—Tripping while disembarking.

—Insulting a guy bigger than you who's waiting for a taxi.

—Not getting a taxi.

CHECK LIST

While waiting for your plane to take off, you might want to give the aircraft a minute inspection to see if it is airworthy. A few points which the pilot might have overlooked during his inspection:

—Are there landing gears?

—Are the oxygen masks hanging down?

—Is the Arabic-speaking man sitting next to you wearing a mask?

—Is your stewardess crying?

—Is a fellow passenger trying to start up "Nearer My God to Thee?"

—Are there FBI men running up to the runway shouting and firing at the tires?

MARCH 12

Science Tells Us . . .

An airplane dropped from a height of one mile will hit the ground at the same time as one cruising at the same height without wings. This astounding fact is based on elementary physics and was stated, in somewhat different language, by Galileo.

MARCH 13

National Poison Prevention Week, March 13–19

HORRORSCOPE: Avoid liquids and solids today.

MARCH 14

Coward's Hall of Shame

Clark Kent

CITATION: For finding it necessary to prove his virility by undressing in a phone booth all the time.

MARCH 15

The Ides of March

Don't go to the Senate today.

MARCH 16

Fear of Blizzard of '88 and Chromosome Damage Day

Chromosome Fears:
—Fear of having fewer than 25 pairs.
—Fear of having greater than 25 pairs.
—Fear of not being sure of what a chromosome is.
—Fear of thinking Chromosome is Zenith's new picture tube.

MARCH 18

From the Annals of Military Cowardice

DEFENSIVE WARFARE: The Great Wall of China was thought to be invincible. Illustration shows how the Mongol Hordes penetrated it.

MARCH 19

HORRORSCOPE: That ugly rumor at the office will prove to be true.

MARCH 20

National Office Fears Week, March 20–27

—Fear of asking for a raise.
—Fear of the boss thinking you want to ask for a raise and firing you.
—Fear of the people at the water cooler gossiping about you.
—Fear of secretaries, file clerks and stock boys.
—Fear that your secretary will get pregnant and try to blackmail you even though you haven't been able to get anywhere with her.
—Fear that you aren't worrying enough about office problems.
—Fear of disagreeing with the boss.
—Fear that if you don't disagree with the boss, he'll think you're not aggressive enough.
—Fear of drinking too many martinis when at lunch with a client.
—Fear of no martinis at lunch.
—Fear of getting in a rut.
—Fear of getting into a valley of fatigue.
—Octophobia (fear of the guy who gets in every morning at eight).

MARCH 22

Second Day of Spring

MARCH 23

Garbage Day

SIGN OF THE DAY

"Caution: Do not puncture or incinerate can."

—Related fear: Fear of not being able to throw away spray
cans.
—Fear of throwing a spray can in the garbage and when the
crusher on the garbage truck hits it, it explodes and cuts one
of the garbage men and he sues you for a million dollars.
—Fear of throwing out something important.
—Fear of allowing too much junk to accumulate because you're
afraid of throwing out something important.

MARCH 25

Coward's Guide to Dining Out

Basic Dining Fears

1. Fear that waiter will speak to you in French.

2. Or, what is worse, that you will speak to him and he won't understand you.

3. Fear of not tipping the maitre d' or the hatcheck girl enough.

4. Fear of mispronouncing the name of a Greek dish so that the waiter thinks you have called him "the son of a sixty-year-old prostitute."

MARCH 28

HORRORSCOPE: The only things you have to fear today are:
  a) getting up
  b) going out
  c) fear itself

MARCH 30

Thought for the Day

That one-in-a-billion shot will occur today! No, you won't win the Irish Sweepstakes. A secretary on the 102nd floor of the Empire State Building will drop her lipstick out of the window, striking you squarely on the head at the speed of an M-16 bullet.

APRIL 1

Fear of being fooled on April Fool's Day, or Aprilfoolophobia, is very common today. So is the fear that nobody will laugh at your April Fool's joke.

APRIL 3

Sex Fears

—Fear of not being a virgin.
—Fear of being a virgin.

APRIL 5

Coward's Hall of Shame

Peter Pan

CITATION: For being afraid of a) his own shadow and b) growing up.

APRIL 6

One of the best-kept medical secrets of our day: *everything* gives white mice cancer.

APRIL 8

Play of the Week: *Who's Afraid of Virginia Woolf?* by Edward Albee

Review: "I was."

APRIL 14-15

Between yesterday and today, the White Star liner *Titanic* hit an iceberg in the North Atlantic in 1912, killing 1,517.

Great Moments in Cowardice

Men leaving the *Titanic* dressed in women's and children's clothes. Exclusive picture not being printed here because of fear statute of limitations may not have run out.

APRIL 15 (MIDNIGHT)

Did your employer take enough withholding tax?

APRIL 16

(Good Friday)

"Thank God it's Friday."
   —Pontius Pilate, ca. A.D. 33

APRIL 18

(Easter Parade)

Fashion Note: White feather introduced on this day, 1753.

APRIL 26

Sex Fears

—Fear of receiving long-distance obscene phone calls. Collect.
—Fear of not receiving any obscene phone calls at all.
—Fear of thinking oral sex means kissing.

MAY 3

The Coward's Hall of Shame

Mantan Moreland

CITATION: For playing the jittery, pop-eyed houseboy in most of those old Charlie Chan movies and for saying "Feets, do yo'h stuff."

MAY 4

Today, being somewhere in the middle of Taurus, is Fear of Astrology Day

Astrological Fears

—Fear of astrology.
—Fear of two strologies.
—Fear of any number of strologies.
—Fear of being born under the wrong sign, like "This Building Is Condemned!"
—Fear of your moon being in someone else's house.
—Fear of your ascendant descending.
—Fear of Venus not making pencils.
—Fear of Mercury poisoning.
—Fear of Jupiter aligning with Mars and you can't get a decent picture on your TV for the next thousand years.
—Fear of heavenly bodies refusing to go out with you.

MAY 5

May 5–11 is National Insect Electrocution Week

MAY 6

Thought for the Day

What have you done to make the Syndicate want to rub you out?

MAY 8

(Fear of Doctors Day)

Mary Morse Baker Eddy's birthday. Founder of Christian
Science, Mrs. Eddy lived for almost a century.

MAY 9

Q. What is a religious coward?
A. A Christian Scientist who secretly belongs to Blue Cross.

MAY 11

(Fear of Falling Objects Day)

—Fear of falling stars.
—Fear of objects falling out of
the fourth, fifth, sixth and
eleventh dimensions.
—Fear that a flaming spot in
the sky above you means that
a long defunct satellite has lost
its orbital momentum and is
about to fall on you.

—Fear of fall (September 21
–December 21)

Thought for the Day:

"Was Chicken Little Right?"

MAY 14

—Fear of not signing your name the same every time.

—Fear of looking different from your picture.

—Fear of no one accepting your collect call.

MAY 23

Ancient Chinese Proverbs

He who look before he leap always keep feet on ground.
He who run away will live to fight another day. So don't stop.
Only brave deserve fair, but only fat, cowardly rich merchant
    can afford.
Brave die only once but student deferment die in bed.

JUNE 1

Fight the Filthy Fly Month, June 1–30

If there is a mosquito buzzing you in your bedroom when you're
trying to sleep your best bet is to quickly enlist in the Navy
and ask to be stationed at Point Barrow, Alaska, where, if the
mosquito has any sense at all, he will not follow you.

Common Fallacies:

Only the female mosquitoes are bothersome.

While it is true that only the female mosquitoes will go to the
trouble of cutting a hole in your skin, sticking in a straw, sucking
out your blood, patching up the hole, injecting an anti-clotting
agent, etc., it's no fun to be in a room full of male mosquitoes
either.

JUNE 4

(Old Maid's Day)

Old Maid Fears

—Fear of a man under your bed.
—Fear of your bed under a man.
—Fear that a man has used your toothbrush and you'll become pregnant.
—Fear of finding a small Eskimo rapist in your refrigerator.
—Fear that you will be violated while riding a man's bicycle.
—Fear of American Legion Conventions in town.
—Fear of the Hell's Angels at all times.

JUNE 7

The Coward's Museum

Chamberlain's Umbrella

JUNE 9

Parental Fears Week, June 9–15

Parental Fears:

—Fear of being a parent.
—Fear of having children.

JUNE 11

M: Now, Harold . . .

S: Yes, Mother?

M: Harold, I want you to unzip my dress.

S: Yes, Mother.

M: Harold?

S: Yes, Mother?

M: Harold, I want you to take off my dress.

S: Yes, Mother.

M: Now, Harold . . .

S: Yes, Mother?

M: I want you to unhook my bra.

S: Yes, Mother.

M: Now, Harold . . .

S: Yes, Mother?

M: I want you to take off my bra.

S: Yes, Mother.

M: Now, Harold . . .

S: Yes, Mother?

M: I want you to take off my panties and look at me.

S: Yes, Mother.

M: Now, Harold . . .

S: Yes, Mother?

M: I don't ever want to catch you wearing my clothes again.

S: Yes, Mother.

JUNE 12

Another Great Moment in Cowardice

The invention of the Conference (A.D. 574 approx.). King
Arthur's Round Table. Originally designed as a strategy for
those who wanted to talk instead of fight, it was later adopted
by business as a means of avoiding decision.

JUNE 14

(Flag Day)

Display the White Flag Proudly!

Excerpts from the Coward's Flag Manual

How to Display the White Flag:
1. From left to right.
2. From top to bottom.
3. If hanging, then to the left.
4. When next to other flags, hidden.
5. If sheets are used, they must not be slept in.
6. The percentage of the flag which is white must not exceed
   100 per cent.

JUNE 20

June 20–26 Is Electric Power Week

The Shocking Story of Electrical Shock

According to the National Safety Council, about 1,000 people
each year lose their lives due to accidental electric shock. This
figure does not include any of those who lose their lives because of intentional electric shock, spiteful electric shock, etc.
It doesn't take much electricity to be lethal. As little as 25 volts
(roughly one quarter of house voltage) at 70 milliamperes
(under one tenth of the current drawn by a 100-watt light
bulb) can be fatal. In fact, 15 to 20 milliamperes can be lethal
under the proper circumstances. This amount of current is
twenty to thirty times less than that drawn by the average
electric typewriter.

HORRORSCOPE: You will probably trip on an electric cord
today.

JUNE 22

HORRORSCOPE: The boss will be open to suggestions today, but not yours.

JUNE 28

The Coward's Museum

Art Exhibit:

Paintings from Picasso's little known Yellow Period.

The Unveiling of Mondrian's painting "Yellow on Yellow."

Brancusi sculpture: "Chicken Egg."

JULY 1

FASHION NOTE: The bulletproof vest was introduced today. Thank you, George Grebe of DeWitt, Nebraska.

JULY 2

(Freedom Day)

The Four Freedoms

—Freedom of speech.
—Freedom of religion.
—Freedom from want.
—Freedom to fear.

JULY 3

(Start of July Fourth Holiday)

HORRORSCOPE: Don't drive this weekend. The roads are unsafe. Fly instead.

JULY 5

(National Physical Fitness Day)

The Coward's Decathlon

Schedule of Events:
1) Hurling epithets
2) Character assassination
3) Leaning over backward
4) Taking to one's heels
5) Throwing a fit (a discus-type object)
6) Six-day back peddling race
7) Gnashing teeth
8) Wrestling with conscience
9) Hiding from facts
10) Ax-grinding
11) Beating a hasty retreat
12) Flying the coop
13) Making tracks
14) Turning the other cheek

JULY 8

The Just-a-minutemen, a patriotic, moderate, passive, militant group was founded on this date in 1967.

Some Facts about the Just-a-minutemen:

FLAG: Yellow doormat with coiled worm and motto:
   Tread on Me.

SLOGAN: "Let me think it over and call you back sometime."

JULY 12

Cowardice is 1 per cent inspiration and 99 per cent fear.
                    —Allegedly told to Napoleon at Waterloo

JULY 15

Take This Emotional Temperature Test:

What does this picture do to you?

1) Hot sweat
2) Cold sweat
3) Afraid to say

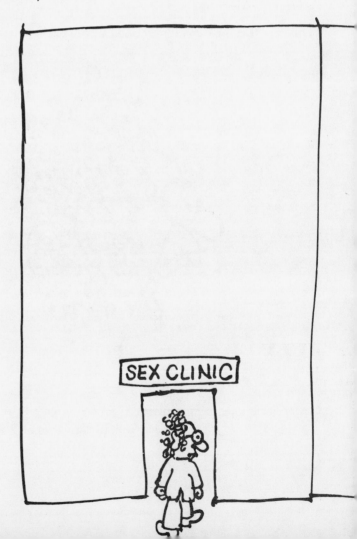

JULY 19

Fear of Computers Month, July 1–31

Computer Fears:

—Fear of accidentally bending, folding or mutilating your card.
—Fear of losing your card.
—Fear of mistakenly substituting a playing card or business card.
—Fear of square holes.
—Fear of seeing increasingly more square holes.
—Fear of waking up in the middle of the night to discover two
  large men standing over you with a square-hole punch.

JULY 22

Law and Order at the Beach

First panel—97-lb. weakling walking on beach with a girl.
Second panel—GIRL: "That bully kicked sand in your face,
  George. What are you going to do?"
Third panel—GEORGE: "I think I'll call a cop."
Fourth panel—Brawny cop leads bully away.
Fifth panel—GEORGE: "Support your local police."

JULY 24

The Dear John Letter

In its simplest form, is:

Dear John,
    Sorry, but I don't love you anymore.

                              Your former friend,
                              Gloria

Its differences from the business flush include the fact that it is
usually (though not always) handwritten in a pretty script,
comes on nice stationery, and may even be perfumed.

    Its similarities include the fact that it, too, comes in many
forms. For example:

Dear Fred,
    I love you, darling. The love I feel for you is so pure and
beautiful that it may last forever. Then there is the other type
of love, the dirty love, the painful love, that may not last, that I
feel for Henry. That's why he and I are getting into this trial
marriage and . . .

Or:

Dear Mike,

You are a really great guy. You know that sculpture that you gave me last week? Well, I showed it to my husband and he agrees that it is really great so . . .

Or:

Dear Ivan,

    Sorry, but I love Frank.

                              Your former friend,
                              Bill

Finally, there is a flush combining the bad points of both the business flush and the Dear John letter:

JULY 25

How to Write a Dear John Letter

Eventually, there comes a time in every coward's life, when he must somehow break off with a former loved one. The Dear John Letter is traditional and should be used. However, a coward cannot merely use one of the forms mentioned yesterday. After all, there are repercussions to consider.

We have come up with some simple rules designed to make the break as clean and simple as possible:

1. *Don't Be Shocking.* You could later be sued for medical expenses incurred because of heart attack or concussion due to hitting the floor too hard after fainting. Better lead up very slowly with an opening like, "Dearest John."
2. *Don't Defame Character.* Insults are nearly always libelous. To be certain that there is no chance of a law suit, fill the letter with compliments like, "You are brave, strong, intelligent, etc."
3. *Avoid Breach of Promise.* This is another lawsuit that's all too easy to get dragged into. Avoid anything similar to breach of promise by pointing out affections like, "I love you. I never want to leave you."
4. *Close on a Cheery Note.* If the victim realizes the intent of the letter too soon, he may set it afire with a cigarette, causing his house to be burned down, also actionable. Best end the letter on a good note like, "Much love, Gloria."

Send the completed letter:

Dearest John,
    You are brave, strong, and intelligent. I love you. I never want to leave you.

                                            Much love,
                                            Gloria

AUGUST 2

HORRORSCOPE: You will find yourself in a compromising position today.

AUGUST 6

(Christopher Marlowe's birthday)

Marlowe is best known in the annals of cowardice for being afraid to sign his name to Shakespeare's plays.

AUGUST 8

Thought for the Day

Is your Italian-American girl friend really giving you the kiss of death?

AUGUST 13

(Friday the Thirteenth)

AUGUST 15

Q. What is the significance of this geometrical progression?
  1) 54–40
  2) 1929
  3) 1984
  4) 38–24–38 (for sexual cowards only)

A. (check one)
  Yes
  No
  Don't know
  Rather not say

AUGUST 19

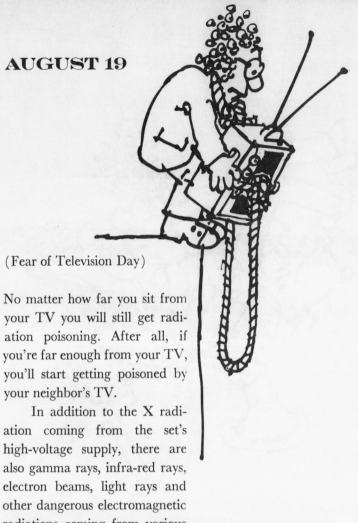

(Fear of Television Day)

No matter how far you sit from your TV you will still get radiation poisoning. After all, if you're far enough from your TV, you'll start getting poisoned by your neighbor's TV.

In addition to the X radiation coming from the set's high-voltage supply, there are also gamma rays, infra-red rays, electron beams, light rays and other dangerous electromagnetic radiations coming from various parts of your television.

Mr. George LeSpart of the World's Finest Television Manufacturing Corporation, Manufacturer of the World's Finest Televisions, claims that there is absolutely no danger to the set owner who follows the prescribed safety procedures. "If you stay at least fifty feet from your set," says Mr. LeSpart, "and wear the proper protective clothing, the worst that can happen to you is that you'll be sterilized. Of course, we haven't analyzed the long-term effects yet."

AUGUST 26

Why Your Fear of Dentists is Well-founded

1) An overdose of novocain can kill.
2) You can choke to death on cotton packing.
3) You can be raped under gas.
4) The high-speed drill can slip and cut off your tongue.

AUGUST 28

The Coward's Consultant

Dear Sir:

    I want to break up with a girl I met last summer. We were very close, and I don't want to do anything to hurt her feelings. Can you suggest what I might say to her in my letter?

                         —Distraught

Dear Distraught:

    A true coward has his mother write the girl a note.

AUGUST 30

The Coward's Hall of Shame

Robert Ford

CITATION: For being that dirty little coward that shot Mister Howard and laid Jesse James in his grave.

SEPTEMBER 1

(Labor Day)

Fear of being replaced by a machine.

SEPTEMBER 3

ACTUARIAL TABLES FOR COMPUTING LIFE EXPECTANCIES
BY PROFESSION

Occupation	Death rate (population in general)	Death rate (cowards)
Test pilots	4.61	0.00
Deep sea divers	3.75	0.00
Mohawk Indians (sky-scraper tribe)*	9.72	0.00
Elevator operators	1.74	0.00
President of the U.S.	4.05	0.00
Unemployed	0.45	0.00

* Includes statistics for drinking on the job.

SEPTEMBER 5

The Coward's Hall of Shame

Melvin Goldfarb

CITATION: For letting his parents continue to pay for his tuition while secretly working in a tie store, intercepting his grade reports in the mail, and sending his earnings to The Universal Free Life Church for a mail-order doctorate, the safe way.

SEPTEMBER 8

Invention of acupuncture in China, 1200 B.C.

First malpractice suit for leaving needle in patient, China, 1200 B.C.

SEPTEMBER 15

Can a Xerox machine sterilize you?

Why do Xerox machines use green light?

Do novelty X-ray "specs" emit dangerous X rays?

How about common household radiators?

Are there dozens of extremely dangerous radiations that have not yet been discovered?

Of course, there are no answers for these questions, but they're something to think about. The most unanswerable of all is why Xerox machines use green light. A spokesman for Xerox claims that it improves contrast and prevents something called "chromatic aberration." Of course, he doesn't know, and was just trying to keep us calm.

SEPTEMBER 23

Definition and Derivation

Courage is grace under pressure.

ERNEST HEMINGWAY

Cowardice is disgrace under pressure.

ANON.

Pressure is Grace under Ernest.

A FRIEND

SEPTEMBER 29

Anniversary of the Shortest Fight, 1946

Al Couture or Ralph Walton, depending how you look at it,
engaged in the shortest prize fight in history—10½ seconds,
including a 10-second count—which ended when Couture
knocked out Walton while the latter was adjusting a gum shield
in his corner (September 29, 1946). The shortest fight of all time,
however, was a welterweight battle on September 2, 1957, when
Teddie Barker of England scored a TKO over Bob Roberts of
Nigeria after the referee stopped the fight following one blow
from Barker.

OCTOBER 2

Today's Sign

Employees Must Wash Hands After Handling Food.
                                        DEPARTMENT OF HEALTH

OCTOBER 4

Stock Tip

Put your money in Bowery Savings at 6 per cent.

OCTOBER 8

From the Annals of Defense

The first ostrich stuck his head in the ground, this being the first documented defensive position, 1,000,000 B.C., today.

Nature Lesson:

Q. Why does the ostrich stick his head in the sand?
A. Where else do you hide in the desert?

OCTOBER 9

Newspaper Fears

—Fear of being quoted incorrectly.

—Fear of your name being spelled wrong.

—Fear of your name being put under somebody else's picture.

—Fear of your picture being put over someone else's name.

—Fear of being quoted correctly, but it's not what you meant to say.

—Fear that they will print lies about you.

—Fear that they will print the truth about you.

—Fear of typographical errors that can change the course of your life.

OCTOBER 13

(Columbus Day)

Fear of Discovery Day

—Fear of discovering a new disease.

—Fear of discovering a new poison and being awarded the Nobel Prize posthumously.

—Fear of making a startling discovery, shouting "Eureka!" and nobody cares because it was discovered centuries ago.

—Fear of shouting "Eureka!" because you don't know what it means.

OCTOBER 15

Tour a Home of the Brave today.
See how the other half lives.

OCTOBER 16

HORRORSCOPE: They said it couldn't be done, but you'll try and find out they were right.

OCTOBER 18

(Don Ameche's birthday)

Bellophobia (fear of telephones)

A ringing phone means trouble. On the other end of the line is
probably:
—A creditor
—A dance studio
—A political candidate
—An obscene caller
—A heavy breather
—A wrong number
—An FBI man
—A mutual fund salesman
—An insurance salesman
—A television-rating service
—A public-opinion poll
—Your son, from jail
—A state policeman, from an accident site
—An airline reporting an overdue flight
—A man saying he's just set off a bomb in your building
—A phone company

OCTOBER 21

Whistles in the Dark

A coward is a hero who has wised up.

ANON.

OCTOBER 27

(Veteran's Day)

Things to do on Veteran's Day

1) Walk with a pronounced limp.
2) Talk a lot about "over there."
3) Use expressions like "my CO," "I was OC," "M-16," "B-52," "ruptured duck," "SNAFU," "Mademoiselle from Armentieres," and "NBC."
4) Walk around with teary eyes.
5) Hide your 4-F classification, ordination certificate, dishonorable discharge, and/or souvenir pocketbook.

NOVEMBER 2

Advice Column

Dear Sir:

 I have a friend who is an artist. She is always asking me what I think of her paintings. I don't have the nerve to say.

        —Critic

Dear Critic:

 When asked to render an opinion on a friend's play, poem, painting, pop song, pottery, etc., you can say:

1) How long did it take you to do it?
2) Whatever gave you the idea, anyway?
3) There's no doubt you put a lot of work into it.
4) It's interesting.

NOVEMBER 5

(Election Day)

Great Moments in Courage (inspirational reading for politicians only)

I will not seek, nor will I accept, a second term.
—Lyndon B. Johnson, March, 1968,
after he lost the New Hampshire primary

NOVEMBER 8

The School of Yellow Journalism was founded on this date. Here are some excerpts from the current reading list:

The Plays of Noel Coward—Coward
Notes on a Cowardly Lion—Lahr
I Am Curious, Yellow—Sjoman
Rabbit, Run—Updike
Catch 22—Heller

"The pen is mightier than the sword!"—The case for prescriptions rather than surgery. "Mightier still is the eraser!"

NOVEMBER 9

Warning: Stay in bed today.

NOVEMBER 10

While Kuru or laughing sickness afflicts only the Fore tribe of Eastern New Guinea, it is 100 per cent fatal. When was the last time you checked to be sure that you have no lineage from the Fore tribe of Eastern New Guinea?

NOVEMBER 14

The Psychological Adviser

Q. I always have this deep-seated fear that if I'm too optimistic, something bad is bound to happen. I am also afraid sometimes that if I am too pessimistic, disaster will become a self-fulfilling prophecy. What am I to do?

A. Nothing. Either way, you're right.

NOVEMBER 17

HORRORSCOPE: Today another golden opportunity will slip through your fingers.

NOVEMBER 18

The Coward's Hall of Shame Juvenile Division

Chicken Little

CITATION: For distinguished contributions to meteorology.

NOVEMBER 20

Thought for the Day

You can be riding the Eighth Avenue subway during the rush hour and anybody can jab your arm with a needle. By the time you reach Forty-second Street you can be a hopeless addict.

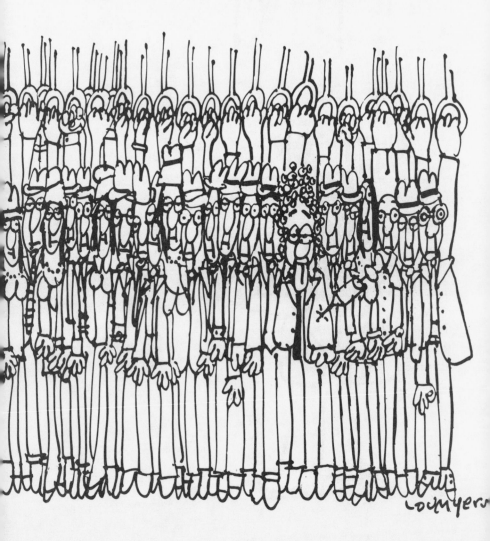

NOVEMBER 24

(Wilbur Craven's birthday)

Wilbur Craven (1465–1551); A Biography

Craven, a lad of sixteen at the time, was the first boy in English history to evidence signs of utter terror when forced to ask a girl out. His symptoms, now commonly known collectively as Craven Cowardice, are discernible by a quivering in the region of the knees, eyes foggy or out of focus, a hollow (sometimes jangling) sensation in the pit of the stomach, lips dry and white, beads of perspiration forming on the forehead when near the opposite sex, and a marked tendency to gather in groups of boys his own age.

Young Wilbur, who was baffled by these sudden signs of inexplicable timidity, performed several experiments on himself to determine the exact cause and nature of the disease, some of which included: waiting until the last possible minute to ask a girl out; walking several miles out of his way to bump into the cutest thing in his Comparative English Lit. class; and dancing with several homely girls in order to work up the courage to ask the pretty one in their midst.

Craven's most painful experiment, and his greatest contribution, was the discovery of the blind date, which he found to be the ultimate in weekend cowardice in that it throws two cowards together for an unspecified amount of time under enormous pressure. The discovery was credited to others.

NOVEMBER 25

Feats of Clay

1) Ensign in the Army of M. DeBourbon who, thinking he had retreated into the city, threw himself into the jaws of the enemy.
2) Battle of Germanicus vs. the Germans, in which both parties were so paralyzed with fear that they ran to the opposing sides.
3) The Carthaginians who, reports Montaigne, were so "affrighted by a panic terror [of the Romans] they ran out of their houses screaming and killed one another."

NOVEMBER 26

"If God wanted us to be brave, why did he give us legs?"

NOVEMBER 27

(Thanksgiving Day)

"What's there to give thanks for, anyway?"

NOVEMBER 29

HORRORSCOPE: Your zip code contains a hidden meaning. You will not discover it.

NOVEMBER 30

The Coward's Hall of Shame

John Alden

CITATION: This one speaks for itself.

DECEMBER 3

Coward's Book Club Selection: *Fear Without Childbirth*

DECEMBER 7

In 1941, the Japanese Military, realizing that America could be caught off guard on Pearl Harbor Day, bombed Pearl Harbor.

"Destiny's Deckhand"

Ichiro L. Kuichi was a simple rice polisher for the Koba Soba Rice Flour Company in Japan. On the day of Pearl Harbor, after the Americans fired on the poor helpless Japanese aircraft which were attacking them, Kuichi joined the Japanese Navy to avenge, as his Emperor put it, "this day of infamy."

His first assignment was as a suicide Kamikaze pilot, but after he had completed ten missions, his superiors decided he had an inadequate death wish. He was kicked out of the Japanese Naval Air Force in disgrace and was assigned as a messboy on his Imperial Emperor's destroyer, *Destiny*.

It was in this capacity that Seaman Fourth Class Kuichi played a role that was to change the course of history, not only in the United States, but in the world. Nobody knew it, but there were two Japanese destroyers coming down the strait that fateful night when John Kennedy was commanding the PT-109. One was the *Destiny* with Seaman Kuichi aboard, and the other was the destroyer that actually rammed the Kennedy boat. The *Destiny* had first crack at ramming the PT-109 but missed because of Seaman Kuichi's behavior under fire.

This is what happened, in Seaman Kuichi's own words: "It was very dark. I on bridge serving green tea to duty officer and helmsman. I very nervous because I know somewhere out there in dark is future President of United States in torpedo boat. I drop tea on duty officer's lap and he yells: 'You stupid fisherman!' In Japanese, that sounds like 'Hard Rudder Right!' Obediently, helmsman swings wheel right instead of ramming PT-109 with future President on board. We miss boat completely and sink PT-110 instead. All crew survived, but nobody important.

"Captain of destroyer is very mad because after war he wants to go into Japanese politics, and he knows it would be very popular issue if he can say he helped future President get elected.

"But it too late. We hear cheers on other Japanese destroyer because they know after war they can sell their story to American magazines and newspapers for millions of yen. Nobody talks to me on my destroyer, because American magazines won't give a bag of rice for how we sank PT-110."

—From the court martial proceedings against
S/4C Ichiro L. Kuichi, Imperial Japanese Navy records

DECEMBER 9

Skiing Instructions

Simply show up at the slopes with a cast on and go directly to the lounge.

DECEMBER 10

HORRORSCOPE: The face you see in the mirror this morning will not be your own.

DECEMBER 11

Today is fear of snow day. Some common fears include:

—Fear of your snowman melting before you have a chance to finish him.
—Fear of being hit by a runaway sled.
—Fear of being drowned when the snow melts.
—Fear of walking in snow higher than the tops of your boots and it falls in.

DECEMBER 13

The Coward's Consultant

Dear Sir:

    I'm a junior in college, and my friends keep calling me chicken because I don't want to use pot or LSD. What should I do?

—With It

Dear Mr. It:

    As I see it, you have two choices. Develop a Christ complex (study Billy Graham's books for authenticity) or walk directly into a wall mumbling "far out" as you do so. Either way, your friends will feel certain you're onto something stronger than they've got. Incidentally, a reasonably safe drug is amino acid. Ask your druggist.

DECEMBER 14

(Lemming's Day)

Today's Worry:

The Population Explosion

DECEMBER 16

Any coward can fight a battle when he's sure of winning; but give me the man who has pluck to fight when he's sure of losing. That's my way, sir; and there are many victories worse than a defeat.

—George Eliot in *Janet's Repentance*

George Eliot was a woman.

DECEMBER 18

Even paranoids have real enemies.

—A generally accepted truth

DECEMBER 19

Coward's Book Club Alternate Selection: *Living Causes Cancer . . .* , the ultimate environmentalist work, by Professor Larry Milord.

DECEMBER 21

—Fear that your neighbor's Christmas decorations are bigger and better than yours.
—Fear of your daughter being molested by a department store Santa Claus.
—Fear of being electrocuted by your decorations.
—Fear that nobody is maintaining the spirit of the holiday.
—Fear of not being sure what the spirit of the holiday is.

DECEMBER 28

The Coward's Hall of Shame

The Entire Town of *High Noon*

CITATION: For being afraid of crime in the streets.

DECEMBER 29

"The meek shall inherit the earth."

The question is, do we want it??

DECEMBER 30

The Coward's Consultant

Dear Arnold:

The other night at a cocktail party a drunk made a pass at my wife. I beat her up (she's much smaller than I am) for leading him on. Where did I go wrong?

—Grass Widower

Dear Grass:

You acted rashly. The proper etiquette would have been to ask the hostess to close the bar.

DECEMBER 31

Beware of the New Year. It could be even worse than this one was.